First published in Great Britain in 2010 by Buster Books,
an imprint of Michael O'Mara Books Limited,
9 Lion Yard, Tremadoc Road, London SW4 7NQ

Written by Jan Payne
Designed by Zoe Quayle
Edited by Elizabeth Scoggins and Jen Wainwright
Production by Joanne Rooke
Cover by Zoe Quayle (from a design by www.blacksheep-uk.com)
Cover illustration by Paul Moran

A CIP catalogue record for this book is available from the British Library

ISBN: 978-1-906082-93-2

2 4 6 8 10 9 7 5 3 1

www.mombooks.com/busterbooks

Printed and bound in Italy by L.E.G.O.

By buying products with an FSC label you are supporting the growth of responsible forest management worldwide. Papers used by Michael O'Mara Books are natural, recyclable products made from wood grown in sustainable forests. The manufacturing processes conform to the environmental regulations of the country of origin.

The BOYS' Annual 2011

Buster Books

CONTENTS

Let's Go!

In this book, you'll discover a boys' world ready to explore.

You'll travel to Ancient China and hunt for treasure. You can cook up some real Australian outback grub perfect for eating around the campfire. Why not grab your skateboard and practise some cool moves, or prepare to be spooked with some terrifying true stories? There's lots to do in these pages, so get strapped in, and prepare for some serious fun!

Float-A-Card

Amaze your friends with this simple card trick – making an ordinary playing card float through the air as if by magic. With a little practice, your audience will be gasping at your astonishing magical skills.

You will need:

- an ordinary playing card • matt sticky tape
- 40 cm of invisible nylon thread used for sewing, or 40 cm of very thin, clear fishing line • scissors.

Preparation

Turn the playing card face down and fold the the nylon thread

or fishing line in half. Tape both ends to the centre of the card, as shown here, and press down firmly.

What you do ...

1. Loop the end of the thread around your middle finger so that about 6 cm hangs between your hand and the card.

2. While you are doing this, chat to your audience to distract them from what you are doing with your hands. Say things like, 'Today I will perform a very

special trick – you'll be amazed!' or, 'Just three people in the world can perform this spectacle, and *I* am one of them!'

3. Hold the card up and show it to your audience. Allow them to see the back very quickly, but not long enough for them to notice the tape.

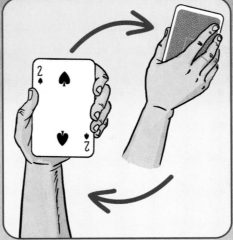

4. Announce that, 'This is a perfectly ordinary playing card, but what you are about to see is incredible – I will make it float and spin through the air!' Make sure you use a very dramatic voice, just like a real magician.

5. As you say, 'through the air', flick the card upwards. Move the hand that is controlling the card up and down a little, to keep the card spinning.

6. At the same time, wiggle the fingers on both hands to make it look as though you are controlling the card by magic.

Weird Nature

The natural world is full of weird and wonderful things, but which of these four amazing stories is just too incredible to be believed? Read each story carefully and try to work out which one of them is a big fat lie. You will find the answer on page 60.

THE BIG STING

You don't want to mess with a swarm of angry bees, but in June 2008, drivers in Canada had no choice. A lorry carrying 330 crates of bees flipped over on a motorway. Thankfully, the driver was not hurt, but a whopping 12 million of his buzzing passengers escaped from their crates.

The bees swarmed all over the road. The more people tried to put them back into their containers, the angrier the bees got, and they started to sting people.

There were so many bees on the loose that the road had to be closed. A team of expert beekeepers worked at getting the furious bees to buzz off back to their containers. To do this, they used a machine called a 'smoker', which puffs out smoke and calms the bees. Bee-lieve it or not, most of the bees were eventually captured and put safely back in their crates.

TRUE OR FALSE?

CLIMBING RABBITS

The fruit of the Moroccan argan tree is an important part of the diet of the local rabbits. These greedy critters are not content to wait for the fruit to fall to the ground, they have learned to climb the trees in order to get to their dinner at its ripest.

You'll often see the trees packed with rabbits. Their claws are long and curved so that they can grip the bark of the tree and climb more easily.

The argan fruit has a stone inside, which the rabbits can't digest. They spit it out and local farmers collect the stones and grind them up to make cooking oil.

TRUE OR FALSE?

LAKE OF DOOM

One hot August day in 1986, people living near a lake in the African country of Cameroon heard a strange bubbling sound. They watched in horror as a huge fountain of water erupted from the lake. This was followed by a foul-smelling cloud that travelled towards them across the surface of the water. When the cloud reached the village, 1,700 people and thousands of birds and animals were killed.

The lake had formed over the crater of a volcano. This deadly cloud was caused by huge amounts of carbon dioxide gas, which had been released into the lake from the volcanic rock and bubbled up through the water.

Scientists have now worked out a way to 'de-gas' the water in the lake. This should stop the killer lake from striking again.

TRUE OR FALSE?

SURF'S UP!

For years, thrill-seeking surfers have travelled to the Amazonian jungle in Brazil, in search of one of the wildest wave-riding experiences nature has to offer.

When an exceptionally high tide in the Atlantic Ocean collides with the Amazon River, a massive wave surges up the river at speeds of up to 30 kilometres per hour. This phenomenon is known as 'Pororoca', which means 'Great Roar'. The sound of the wave is so loud you can hear it coming half an hour before it appears, ripping up trees and flattening houses.

To ride the powerful Pororoca is every surfer's dream. The wave can reach almost 9 metres high, and skilful surfers can ride it for many kilometres at a time. The very best surfers can keep going without falling off their boards for more than 30 minutes!

TRUE OR FALSE?

Special Effects

If you see a film which has special effects, you want them to look realistic – the blood should look like blood and the slime should look like slime. However, you don't need to go to Hollywood to become a special effects wizard. Follow these easy steps to make your own truly spooky look to freak out your friends.

THE BLOODTHIRSTY VAMPIRE!

You will need:

- a selection of face paints • a black eyeliner pencil
- 1 tbsp golden syrup • ½ tsp red food colouring • a few drops of blue food colouring • a pinch of plain flour
- vampire teeth (from fancy dress shops or joke shops).

Top tip

All of these scary effects can be easily removed with warm, soapy water.

What you do ...

1. Using your fingers, cover your whole face with a layer of white face paint.

2. Dab red face paint on your eyelids and around the eyes. Then add it to your cheeks and blend it down to your jaw-line. Gently rub with your fingers so you don't look too stripy!

3. Carefully draw a line of black eyeliner under each eye. Then draw a black V-shape on your forehead, as shown below. This is called a widow's peak and all vampires have them.

5. Dip the ends of the vampire fangs into the fake blood mixture before putting them in your mouth. Finally, smear some blood around your mouth for a terrifying finishing touch!

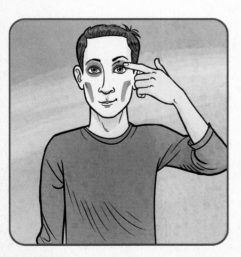

4. Now it's time to make your fake blood. Mix the syrup in a bowl with the red and blue food colouring to create a sticky, dark red liquid. Add the flour and stir it in so that the blood thickens.

HOW TO FAKE A CUT

You will need:
- make-up remover and a piece of cotton wool • PVA glue
- liquid foundation make-up (see if you can borrow some)
- a tissue or sheet of toilet paper • scissors • a paintbrush
- a blunt pencil • red water-based art paint.

What you do ...

1. Use make-up remover and cotton wool to clean the area of skin where you want your 'cut'.

2. Cut 4 to 5 pieces of tissue, measuring roughly 2 cm by 6 cm.

3. Pour a tablespoon of PVA glue into a small bowl and add a pea-sized blob of foundation.

4. Mix together thoroughly using the wrong end of your pencil, so your glue looks flesh-coloured.

5. Paint a thin layer of fleshy glue on the clean area of skin, about the same size as the tissue pieces.

6. Place a piece of tissue over the fleshy glue and gently press it down with the paintbrush.

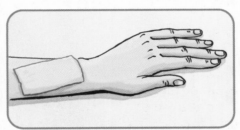

7. Repeat steps **5** and **6** until you have used up the tissue pieces and they blend with your skin.

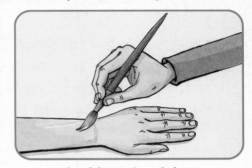

8. Use the blunt tip of the pencil to draw a thin line gently through the glue. Fill in the line with red paint to make it look open and sore.

9. Paint a final layer of fleshy glue around the 'cut' and leave to dry.

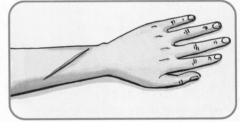

MAKE A BURN SCAR

You will need:
- make-up remover and a piece of cotton wool • liquid foundation make-up (see if you can borrow some)
- PVA glue • a tissue or sheet of toilet paper • scissors
- a paintbrush • a pencil • petroleum jelly.

What you do ...

1. Use make-up remover and cotton wool to clean the area of skin where you want your 'burn'.

2. Cut out several pieces of tissue, roughly the size you want your 'burn' to be.

3. Pour a tablespoon of PVA glue into a small bowl and add a pea-sized blob of foundation.

4. Mix together thoroughly using the wrong end of your pencil, so your glue looks flesh-coloured.

5. Paint a thin layer of fleshy glue on the clean area of skin, the same size as the tissue pieces and press in a piece of tissue using the paintbrush.

6. Repeat until all the tissue pieces are gone, then use your finger to dab at the surface, so that it wrinkles up. This creates a 'puckered', burnt effect.

7. Once the 'burn' is dry, dab petroleum jelly over it with your finger, to make it look really sore.

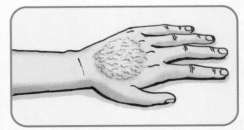

Quiet On Set!

On a film set, the clapperboard shows details of the scene that's about to be filmed. It is snapped shut at the beginning of each scene so that the sound and picture are lined up perfectly. You can make your very own clapperboard to leave important messages for your family outside your door.

What you do ...

1. Remove the shoe box lid and put it aside. This will be the main body of your clapperboard.

2. Take the rest of the box apart and lay it flat. Use your scissors to cut off one of the box's long sides. This card strip will form the 'clapper'.

3. Now measure the depth of the shoe box lid.

You will need:
- a shoe box • a pencil • a ruler • scissors • a stapler
- a glue stick • a sheet of paper • sheets of newspaper
- a large paintbrush • a small paintbrush • blackboard paint • white acrylic paint • chalk.

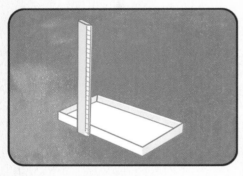

4. Use this measurement to draw three long lines on the card strip, the same width apart as the depth of the lid. If your lid is 2 cm deep, for example, draw three long lines, 2 cm apart.

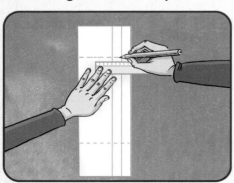

5. Now draw two lines, parallel with the folds, where the corners of the shoebox were, as shown below. Use the depth of the box lid again – 2 cm for instance.

6. Trim off any excess card outside of these marks.

7. Now you need to score the card along each of the long lines you have drawn to make it fold easily. Do this by holding your ruler in place and drawing the tip of your pencil along each long line, so that it dents the card.

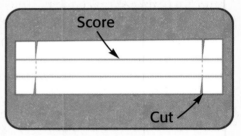

Score

Cut

8. Cut the card to the middle strip, as shown above. Be careful not to cut all the way though! You'll need to do this four times.

9. Fold up the card strip, as shown below. Tuck the flaps inside and staple them in place.

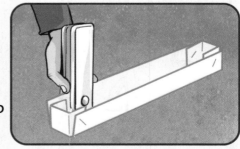

10. Now it's time to join the clapper to the main board. To do this, cut two strips of paper the same width as the clapper and measuring roughly 8 cm long.

11. Place the clapper on top of the board and glue one strip of paper over the join on the left side, as shown below.

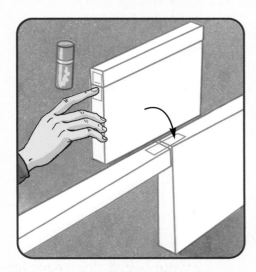

12. Carefully fold back the clapper and glue the other strip over the join on the inside. Fold the clapper back down and leave to dry.

13. Once the clapper is dry, lay out several sheets of newspaper to cover your working surface. Paint the whole clapperboard with the blackboard paint using the large paintbrush and leave to dry.

14. Once dry, carefully use the small paintbrush to paint on the markings, shown here in white acrylic paint.

Using your clapperboard

On a film set, each section of a clapperboard is labelled with things such as the name of the film, the director, the date, the scene number and so on.

Why not label your clapperboard your own way? For example, you could label it with your name, the date, where you are, notes or even what you'd like for breakfast!

Prop the clapperboard up outside your bedroom door, whenever you want to leave everyone a message.

Stunt-Fighting Spirit

A stunt fight is a pretend fight. Nobody gets hurt and every punch or kick is rehearsed over and over again, like a dance routine. Practise this sequence of moves to create a realistic-looking, but totally fake fight.

Before you start ...

… read these tips to make sure your stunt fight goes off without a hitch.

• Make sure you use a soft surface – either grass, or a carpeted floor.

• Don't get too close to your partner – keep a safe distance so that you never actually touch each other.

• Practise each move very slowly until you are getting the hang of it and speed up gradually.

• Only attempt the moves shown here to be certain of a safe stunt fight.

• Practise falling in slow motion, starting with your knees bent, so that you don't hit the ground awkwardly.

Never practise any of these moves if the other person isn't in the know. If they haven't practised with you, they will not know how or when to move and may get hurt.

KNEE NUDGER

1. Stand by your partner's side, put your hands on his shoulders and look him in the eye. This is the signal that you are about to do the Knee Nudger.

2. Turn your partner so that he is side-on to you, with his back to the audience.

3. Your partner should place his right hand on top of his left hand, and bring them both up level with his belly button.

4. Slowly lift your right knee, bringing it level with the height of his stomach.

5. As you lift your knee, your partner should move his hands

gently down to meet it. This will make a thumping sound, as though your knee really has collided with his stomach.

6. At this point, your partner should bend forwards and jump backwards at the same time. This move will need a little practice, but will really convince the audience. 'Ouch!'

PACKING A PUNCH

1. Start by facing your partner, with your back towards your audience.

2. Slowly swing your fist towards the space at the side of your partner's face. Leave a gap of at least 10 cm to make sure you don't make contact.

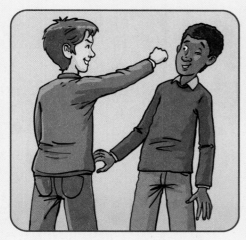

3. As you reach the space to the side of your partner's face, slap your chest with your other hand to make the sound of a 'punch'.

4. At the same time, your partner should stagger back dramatically, as though he has been hit, before you go into your next move.

DEFENCE, DEFENCE!

Let your partner try these two alternate endings to 'Packing A Punch'. Make sure that you plan your moves ahead so that you both know what is coming next!

• As you swing towards him, your partner should move his body in the opposite direction.

Then, as he comes up from his defensive duck, you can move smoothly into another move.

• As an alternative, your partner should use his forearm to push your arm gently away.

Use your eyes to signal to each other which move will be coming next.

Stunt-fight secrets

Once you've mastered these moves, plan a stunt-fight routine with your partner. Make sure that both of you know exactly what order you will do the moves in, as you go through the 'fight'. Practise the whole routine in slow motion, before gradually speeding up.

Let your partner know what you are going to do by 'signalling' your moves. Do this by making a slight movement of your hand or foot which he can see but a watching audience can't.

'Synchronize' your moves so that both you and your partner act at the same time – if you throw a punch, your partner should react to the punch at the same time. This takes a lot of practise to get right, but it will be worth it!

Remember to react dramatically – practise making grunting and groaning noises, and jumping backwards at the right time to make your fight convincing. It's up to you to convince the audience that these fake moves really hurt!

Scary Stories

These terrifying true stories are not for the faint hearted. Read these pages – if you dare!

THE THREE WITCHES

In the 1600s and earlier, women who behaved oddly or lived alone were sometimes thought to be witches. If something unusual happened, such as an unexplained death, it was not uncommon for these 'witches' to be tried and put to death!

Hanged

In 1682, three elderly women from a town in southwest England were accused of witchcraft. The strange illnesses of two other women were said to have been caused by them. So Temperance Lloyd, Susannah Edwards and Mary Trembles were tried for witchcraft and hanged. It was one of the last times that 'witches' were hanged in England.

The ghosts of these women are said to have been seen haunting the prison in which they were held.

THE SECRET CHAMBER

Glamis (pronounced 'glahms') Castle in Scotland is often said to be the most haunted place in Britain. Over the centuries, many terrible things are supposed to have happened there. People have reported hearing strange, unexplainable noises and some even say they have seen mysterious figures in and around the castle grounds.

Strange sounds from a hidden room.

As well as all these ghostly goings-on it is thought that somewhere within the castle lies a mysterious secret chamber locked up for as long as 200 years!

A group of visitors once attempted to discover the location of the chamber by hanging a towel out of every window they could find. However, when they went outside to check where the chamber could be, there was more than one window that did not have a towel showing!

The chamber has never been discovered!

Rumours about why the room would have been locked up vary. Lots of people believe that a child was born to the family who was so deformed that people actually thought he was a monster! He was locked up in the secret chamber and taken for walks at night along a hidden passageway.

Other people believe that several members of a family that came to the castle for help were locked up in the chamber until they died. Later, horrible noises were heard coming from the chamber. It's said that several skeletons were found inside and the room was then locked up for ever.

No nightmares

Although there are many reportings of ghostly sightings and horrible hauntings, scientists have never been able to prove that ghosts really exist. So you can spook your friends with these scary stories and still have a good night's sleep!

THE HEADLESS HORSEMAN

On a cold New Year's Eve in Tarrytown, America, a Dutchman walked home past the Sleepy Hollow cemetery. It was midnight, there was snow on the ground and there was no moon. The only light came from the lantern he was carrying. As he neared the cemetery he noticed a white mist rising from one of the graves. The mist grew and grew and gradually took the shape of a large horse which began galloping towards him. On the back of the horse was a headless rider.

A wounded soldier

Terrified, the Dutchman ran towards a bridge. He knew that ghosts don't like crossing over water. But he stumbled on a patch of melting snow and, as the horse galloped past him, he noticed the rider was wearing a soldier's uniform.

He will search for ever

The story goes that the soldier had lost his head during the Battle of White Plains during the American War of Independence in the 18th century. It was blown off by a cannonball. The soldier's ghost is said to rise from his grave every night to look for it.

The Haunted House

Do you have the nerve to complete these spine-tingling puzzles?
You'll find the answers on page 60.

Enter Here

Exit Here

THE ROOM OF MYSTERIES

Make your way around the objects to reach the exit. You may only cross paths with one frog, one spider and one bat on your way out.

Frog   Spider   Bat

SPOOKDOKU!

To complete the puzzle, fill each empty box with 1, 2, 3 or 4. Every row, column, and smaller box of 4 squares can only contain each number once. Good luck!

1	4	2	3
2	3	1	4
3	2	3	2
4	1	4	1

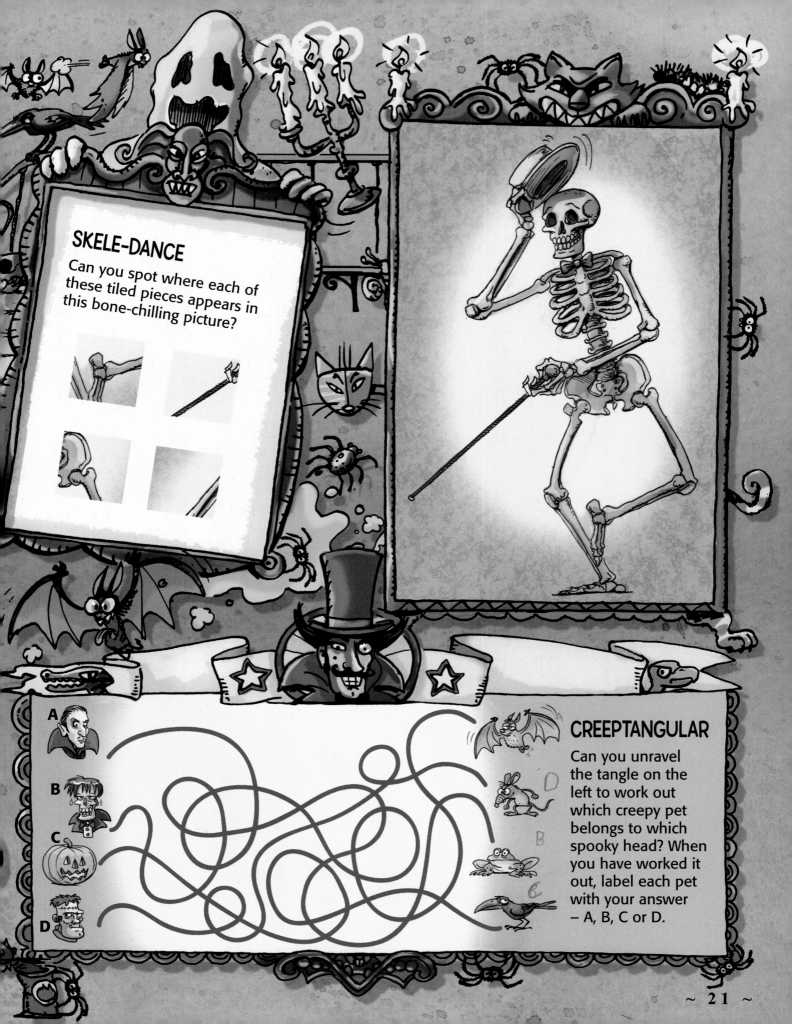

SKELE-DANCE

Can you spot where each of these tiled pieces appears in this bone-chilling picture?

CREEPTANGULAR

Can you unravel the tangle on the left to work out which creepy pet belongs to which spooky head? When you have worked it out, label each pet with your answer – A, B, C or D.

A

B

C

D

~ 21 ~

Outback Puzzler

Can you spot ten differences between these two outback scenes?
Answers on page 60.

Outback Adventure

A picnic in the Australian outback turns to terror for Jack and his aunt, Beatrice. When his aunt is injured, can Jack save the day?

Jack McIntyre was on holiday, visiting his aunt Beatrice who lived in Australia. They were driving through the outback on their way to a town called Alice Springs. The drive was hot, dry and dusty, not to mention long. The outback was so empty they hadn't seen any other cars at all.

'Let's have our picnic before it gets too hot,' said aunt Beatrice, stopping near a tall mound of rock.

'Why don't we climb the rock first?' said Jack.

'Good idea,' said his aunt, putting back the picnic stuff. 'We might be able to see the Aboriginal village from there.' Aborigines are the native people of Australia, who have lived there for thousands of years. They know how to handle the hot desert of the outback better than anyone.

Distant fires

Jack and his aunt climbed to the top of the rock and stood, out of breath, at the top. The view was amazing. Jack had never seen such a colourful landscape. In the distance, they could see the smoke from the fires the Aborigines were using to cook. Jack heard his stomach start to rumble, he was looking forward to their picnic.

Just then, the sound of snarling drifted up to them. Aunt Beatrice's head snapped round at the noise.

A pack of hungry wild dogs called dingoes were fighting at the spot where the car was parked.

'Oh no!' Aunt Beatrice cried. 'The food.' She began to run down the side of the mound of rock. 'Clear off!' she yelled, waving her arms. Suddenly, to Jack's horror, she lost her footing and, half-falling, half-rolling, landed with a thud on the ground.

The dingoes crept away and Jack ran to his aunt as fast as he could. She was lying on the ground with her eyes shut and a deep gash on the side of her head. Jack realized she was unconscious and, for a moment, his mind went blank. Then he jumped into action. Jack knew that he needed to keep his aunt out of the sun and that she would need water when she came round.

Disaster!

He ran to the car for water. To his dismay he saw that the dingoes had eaten all the food. All but one of the bottles of water had leaked everywhere – the last trickles were draining away into the dust.

Jack quickly grabbed the picnic blanket and the last of the water before running back to where his aunt lay. He draped the blanket over some overhanging bushes to shade her from the hot sun and ran out to the road to try to flag down a passing car. They needed help, and soon!

The road was empty. Jack grew more and more worried – he had no food, only enough water for a few hours and the sun was getting hotter. He had read about people being lost in the outback who had to eat snakes and lizards to survive! The thought made him feel sick.

Signalling for help

He climbed back up the rock. He could see the village clearly. But there was no sign of anything moving. Not a person or even a dog, only the plumes of smoke from the campfires in the Aboriginal village.

'That's it,' he thought, 'a fire!' With a smile, he remembered the box of matches in the glove compartment of the car. Aunt Beatrice had brought them in case they had car trouble and needed to make camp for the night. Jack set about gathering sticks and building a small campfire on the top of the rock, making sure it was contained within a circle of smaller rocks. Soon, there was a crackling fire and a plume of white smoke rising into the sky.

It was now so hot that the plain below seemed to shimmer. It was difficult to make anything out, but Jack knew he had to do everything he could. He took off his T-shirt, tied it to a stick and began waving it. 'HELP!' he shouted. 'HELP!'

Suddenly, he spotted a slim figure running towards him. It was a boy from the village. The boy waved at Jack and grinned. Jack clambered down the rock to meet him. The boy was tall and lean. Jack guessed he was about 18 years old. 'I'm Matari,' he said, with a smile.

'I'm so glad to see you,' said Jack with relief. 'My aunt is hurt and I don't know what to do.'

'We must take her to the village,' said Matari when he saw her. 'There's no time to lose.' Together, they lifted aunt Beatrice into the back of the car. Her eyes flickered open and she smiled weakly at Jack. He sat with her, keeping her head supported, as Matari drove back to his village.

Matari's father was the village doctor. He had the same smile as his son. Jack immediately felt at ease when he saw him. The doctor looked at aunt Beatrice and gently cleaned the wound on her head and rubbed in a mixture made from plants to help it heal.

'Your aunt is going to be fine,' he told Jack. 'She just needs to rest. I'll keep an eye on her overnight. You've had a long day – get some sleep.'

Camping out

That night, while his aunt slept in a comfortable bed, Jack and his new friend Matari slept by a campfire. It was an amazing experience sleeping out in the open in the Australian outback. The sky was so black and the millions of stars were as bright as diamonds. Jack sighed happily – despite everything, he'd had an incredible day.

Bush Tucker

Whip up this simple recipe, so that you're never without a delicious snack while exploring the outback.

BILLYCAN BUN

A billycan is a tin used to carry water and to cook things in, like this tasty pudding. If you don't have your own billycan you can still make a Billycan Bun at home. Here's how:

You will need:

- a tea bag • 150 g raisins
- 50 g sultanas
- 100 g sugar
- 225 g flour
- 1 tsp bicarbonate of soda
- 1 tsp mixed spice
- 450 ml boiling water
- a little butter for greasing.

Warning!

When using boiling water, ovens and sharp knives, ask an adult to help you.

What you do ...

1. Preheat the oven to 160°C / Gas Mark 3, then boil the kettle. Measure 450 ml of boiling water into a jug, add the tea bag, stir with a metal spoon and leave to stand.

2. Stir together the raisins, sultanas, sugar, flour, bicarbonate of soda and mixed spice in a large mixing bowl.

3. Remove the tea bag from the jug using the spoon and carefully pour the hot tea over the dry ingredients. Stir until the mixture is smooth.

4. Grease a large loaf tin with a thin layer of butter using a piece of greaseproof paper.

5. Tip the mixture into the tin and bake for about 30 minutes. Ask an adult to help you remove it from the oven and turn it out on to a wire rack to cool. Once cool, cut it into slices and serve.

How To Haka

The Haka is a traditional chanting dance of New Zealand's native Maori people. The New Zealand rugby team, the All Blacks, use it as a challenge at the start of each match.

WHAT'S IT ALL ABOUT?

The words to the traditional 'Ka Mate' Haka tell of a brave leader, taking risks for other people. It is adapted for different ceremonial occasions and, when you use it as a challenge at sporting events, it can be quite impressive if you do it properly!

The words below have been written out as you should pronounce them. Shout them out and make each movement as you shout the words in *italics*. Start with your arms held out horizontally in front of you, bent at the elbows. Make a fierce expression, like a warrior, let your tongue hang out, then follow these instructions:

The 'Ka Mate' translated

This is what the words of the *Ka Mate* Haka mean in English.

It is death, it is death!
It is life, it is life!
I die, I die! I live, I live!
This is the hairy man,
    who fetched the sun
And caused it to shine again.
One upward step,
    another upward step
An upward step,
    another upward step.
The sun shines!

1. Shout: '*Kah* mah teh, *kah* mah teh*,' slapping your thighs on 'kah'.

2. Look fierce and slap your chest as you shout: '*Kow* rah!'

3. Shout: '*Kow* rah!' again, lifting your hands to the sky. Repeat steps **1** to **3**.

4. Punch forwards with your right hand, then your left, shouting: '*Teh* ney teh, *tahn* gata.'

5. Slide your right hand across your body, from hip to thigh, as you shout: '*Pou* hou rou.'

6. Repeat the move several times, chanting: '*Hou* rou. *Nah* nah neh ee tee my. *Phah* kah phee tee teh rah.'

7. Whack your left arm and shout: '*Ah* ou pah neh.' Then switch arms and shout: '*Kah* ou pah neh.'

8. Repeat, changing the shout to: 'Ah *ou* pah neh, kah *ou* pah neh.'

9. Bring your right hand round to your left elbow in a circle, saying: 'Phee tee.'

10. Shout: 'Teh rah!' Look up to your right and place your left hand on your hip.

11. Slap your thighs again, then jump up, shouting: '*He!*'

Top tip

Don't worry about pulling silly faces – the more effort you put into it, the more convincing you will be!

Get On The Pitch

Tag rugby is a simpler and less physical version of official rugby that is suitable for young players. Why not organize a game with some friends at your local park? Here is a simplified version of the game to get you started.

THE BASICS

Teams each have seven players on the pitch at one time. If you have 'spare' players, someone must come off before one can go on.

A game lasts 40 minutes, with a break at half-time.

One point is scored for each 'try', where a player takes the ball over the try line.

Instead of tackling the player who has the ball, as you would in regular rugby, players 'tag'. This is gentler and safer than a real rugby tackle, where players are allowed to pull each other to the ground!

THE PITCH

Pitch sizes vary slightly, but you can easily mark out an area of grass at the park – you just need a centre spot and two try lines, roughly 60 metres apart.

Try Line

Roughly 60 metres

Try Line (roughly 30 metres)

HOW TO PLAY

1. Toss a coin to decide which team starts.

2. To start, stand on the centre spot, hold the ball in both hands and throw it to another player on your team. When you pass the ball to another player, you may only throw it to the side, or behind you, you cannot pass it forwards (in the direction of the opposing team's try line).

3. To get the ball from the opposing team, you must 'tag' the player with the ball by gently tapping him with your hand at waist height, as you would in a playground game of tag. When the opposing team has been tagged five times, they must give you the ball.

TAGGING NOTE. In organized games, fabric tags are used that pull off when a player is tagged.

4. If you are tagged, you must stop running and pass the ball to another player on your team within three seconds. In that time, members of the opposing team have to stay at least one metre away from you, to give you room.

5. If you make it to the opposing team's try line with the ball, place it on or behind the line to score a point. If you are playing on a hard surface, lift the ball up in the air and shout, 'Try!' so that everyone can hear.

6. To re-start the game after scoring a try, or after someone has passed or dropped the ball forwards, in the direction of the opposing team's try line, play a free pass, as you did to start the game, see step **2**. It should be taken from the centre spot if a try has been scored or from the point where the ball dropped on the ground.

Sporty Snacks

Athletes need healthy, high-energy foods to keep them feeling fit and ready to tackle anything. These snack recipes are simple to make and delicious to eat – whether you've had a hard day playing sports or a tough day in front of the TV!

MUNCHABLE MUESLI

You will need:
- 400 g porridge oats • 50 g wheat bran
- 50 g oat bran • 150 g raisins, dried cranberries, dried apricots, or sultanas • 50 g flaked almonds
- 25 g chopped walnuts • 25 g sunflower seeds
- 25 g desiccated coconut.

What you do ...

1. Measure out the ingredients and put them all in a large mixing bowl.

2. Stir them all together until they are well mixed, then pour yourself a small bowlful.

3. Top your bowl up with ice-cold milk, or a spoonful of yogurt, and enjoy your tasty muesli.

4. Put the rest of your muesli mix in an airtight container and store it somewhere cool and dry. It will keep for up to a month.

EASY-PEASY SMOOTHIE

You will need:
- 1 large banana • 250 ml chilled orange juice
- 75 g plain fat-free yogurt
- 4 ice cubes
- 1 tbsp honey.

What you do ...

1. Peel and cut the banana into slices. Put the slices in the freezer and leave them for an hour.

2. Once the banana is frozen, put it in a blender with the yogurt, orange juice, ice cubes and honey. Make sure the lid is on tightly, then blend everything together until it's nice and smooth.

3. Divide the refreshing smoothie between two glasses and share with a friend.

Top tip
Add a spoonful of honey or some chopped fresh fruit to your muesli to give it extra punch.

Warning!
Be sure to warn people that the muesli contains nuts before they try it – some people might be allergic to them.

Kitchen Science

Turn your kitchen into a laboratory with these simple and fun experiments.

ACID OR ALKALI?

In this experiment you can test liquids to find out if they are 'acid' or 'alkali'. Acidic liquids such as lemon juice and vinegar are quite weak, but really strong acids can eat through metal! Acids and alkalis are opposites. Alkalis such as bicarbonate of soda are sometimes used for cleaning.

You can make your own testing kit at home out of nothing more than red cabbage and water. You can then use your kit to find out whether a liquid is acid or alkali in this amazing experiment. Here's how:

You will need:
• half a red cabbage • several empty glass jars • various liquids to test, such as lemon juice, vinegar, cola and washing-up liquid. Dissolve a teaspoon of various non-liquid substances, such as bicarbonate of soda or toothpaste, in some water. Pour each liquid into a separate jar to about 1 cm deep and label each one.

6. When the purple testing liquid is added to different substances, it should change colour dramatically.

What you do ...

1. Chop the cabbage into small pieces and put it into a saucepan. Cover it with water.

2. Ask an adult to help you bring the water to the boil, then turn down the heat, so that the water simmers (bubbles gently). Simmer the cabbage for 20 minutes.

IMPORTANT NOTE. Once the cabbage is cooked, make sure you do not pour the water away – this is the bit you want to keep – although you can eat the cabbage, too!

3. Get an adult to help you strain the cabbage water out into a jug. The water should be dark purple by now. This is your testing liquid.

4. Once the testing liquid has cooled, line up your labelled jars of substances on the kitchen counter.

5. Now it's time to test each of your substances. Do this by pouring a little testing liquid into the first jar and look to see what happens.

7. Lastly, see if you can change the colour of the substances in each jar back again by adding either an acid or an alkali.

SCIENCE STUFF:

Your purple testing liquid is neither acid nor alkali. When you use it to test an acid, it will turn the liquid bright red, and when you use it to test an alkali it will turn the liquid greeny-blue.

STRANGE CELERY STRIPES

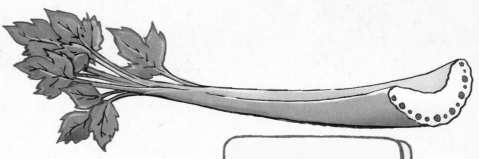

You will need:
- celery, with leaves on top
- food colouring • a glass jar.

What you do ...

1. First pour 1 cm of food colouring into the bottom of the jar.

2. Take a long stalk of celery and cut it across the bottom, at the root end. Place it in the jar. The cut should be covered by the food colouring. Leave it there for half an hour to an hour.

3. Check every so often to see what's happening – you should notice the leaves changing colour.

4. Carefully pour the food colouring away and rinse off the end of the celery.

5. Lastly, enjoy a nice colourful snack – it goes brilliantly with peanut butter.

SCIENCE STUFF:

When you bite or cut the celery, you'll see lots of coloured stripes running up the inside of the stalk to the leaves. This is because, even when a celery stalk has been cut from its roots in the ground, it can still draw liquid through its 'vessels' – the tubes that carry water through the plant.

THE INCREDIBLE BOUNCING EGG!

You will need:
- a hard-boiled egg • vinegar – any will do, but white vinegar will make it easier to see what's going on • an old glass jar.

What you do ...

1. Ask an adult to hard boil an egg for you. Then, once it is cool enough to touch, place the egg in the jar and pour in enough vinegar to cover it. Don't worry if the egg has cracked in the pan – it won't matter as long as no egg has leaked out.

2. After a few minutes, you'll start to notice a few changes – tiny bubbles will start to appear all over the shell – it may even start to spin in the vinegar!

3. Wait half an hour and then gently rub the shell with your finger – it should start to come off quite easily. Put the egg back.

4. Put the jar in an out-of-the-way place where it won't get knocked over – you'll need to leave the egg for three days to get the bounciest results.

5. After three days in the vinegar, rinse any remaining shell off the egg under a running tap.

You'll be left with a rubbery, bouncy, unpredictable eggy toy. Don't eat it though!

SCIENCE STUFF:

Eggshell is made of a substance called calcium carbonate. The acid in the vinegar eats away at it and leaves the egg rubbery at the same time.

Useless Inventions

Have you ever had an idea for an invention, but thought it was just too silly? Check out the bonkers brainwaves below. Ten of them are real inventions, two of them are sneaky lies – can you guess which? Answers on page 60.

FORK ALARM

Everyone knows that you should chew your food properly before you swallow it, but the Fork Alarm makes sure you never forget. It has buzzers and flashing lights to tell you when it's okay to fork in another mouthful.

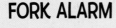

TRUE OR FALSE?

INCY-WINCY SPIDER LIBERATOR

This tiny ladder attaches to the side of your bath. Any spiders that fall in can use it to climb their way out and scuttle to safety.

TRUE OR FALSE?

DOGGLES ®

Cool sunglasses for cool dogs! On a bright day these clever shades prevent the sun getting in your pet's eyes. Good for keeping the dirt out when he's digging a hole, too!

TRUE OR FALSE?

TROUSER CHAIR

These stylish trousers have a hidden pull-cord. Pull it and they inflate, providing you with a comfortable chair, wherever you are.

TRUE OR FALSE?

HOT-AIR EAR DRYER

If you think a towel is all you need to dry yourself after swimming, think again. Slot this machine into your ear after swimming and the hot air will gently blow your ears dry.

TRUE OR FALSE?

SANTA DETECTOR

This special Christmas stocking can be hung above your fireplace and has a series of lights hidden on it that flash brightly when Santa Claus comes down the chimney.

TRUE OR FALSE?

GLASS COFFIN

A man from New York thought it would be nicer to encase a dead person in solid glass rather than bury them. The coffin could then stand in the corner of the living room for everyone to admire. Spooky!

TRUE OR FALSE?

FISH TOILET

This invention is a toilet and fish bowl in one. These incredible poop-munching perch are housed in a special transparent toilet bowl, eating anything you'd usually flush away. The perfect pet to help you save the planet!

TRUE OR FALSE?

MOUSTACHE CUP

Bushy moustaches were very popular in Victorian times, but drinking tea made moustaches very soggy. The moustache cup was invented to fight this problem. These teacups were fitted with a moustache-shaped ledge that let the drinker enjoy his tea, while his facial hair stayed dry.

TRUE OR FALSE?

AIR-CONDITIONED SHOES

Say goodbye to smelly feet. This contraption is fitted into the heels of your shoes. The pressure you put on your heels as you walk powers the cooling system within, keeping your feet fresh and cool.

TRUE OR FALSE?

SCREAM MUFFLER

Life can make you want to scream, really LOUDLY. With the scream muffler, you can yell as loudly as you like without worrying about disturbing anyone. It is a tube that you put over your mouth, which is filled with a sound-absorbing foam.

TRUE OR FALSE?

PAT ON THE BACK MACHINE

Sometimes you need to feel like your hard work has been appreciated in order to feel better. With this handy machine, you can literally give yourself a pat on the back – rewarding yourself for whatever it is you have done.

TRUE OR FALSE?

Manga Mayhem

Manga is a style of drawing that began in Japanese comic books. Now it's one of the most popular drawing styles in the world. Read on to learn how to 'Manga' yourself.

You will need:
- a full-length photograph of you in which you are standing quite straight and facing the camera – it helps if the photo is a close-up and clear • several sheets of paper • a pencil
- a black felt-tip pen • an eraser.

1. Draw a circle for your head.

2. Then look at your chin in the photo. Is it round, square or pointed?

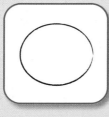

Add a round, square or pointed line below the circle.

3. Draw a long line down from your chin, about twice as long as the whole head. Don't worry if it isn't too straight. This is your backbone.

4. Leave a small gap below the head and add an oblong. This will be the shoulders. Leave a gap for your waist and draw another oblong for the hips.

5. Leave a space below your hips roughly the length of your head and draw two small circles. These are your knees.

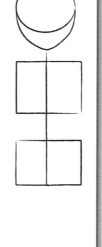

6. Do the same again for your ankles, then add two small circles, either side of your waist to make your elbows.

Add two small circles either side of the bottom of the hips to make your wrists.

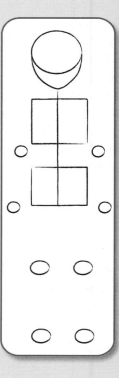

7. Draw joining lines between the outside of the ankles, knees and hips and the outside of the wrists, elbows and shoulders. Then do the same on the insides, like this. Don't forget to add lines for your waist, too.

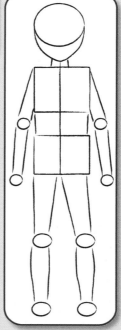

Top tip
Draw all your pencil lines quite lightly, as you will need to be able to rub them out later, once you have gone over them in pen.

8. Large feet are really important to create a Manga style. Add a big oval around each ankles – don't be afraid to go huge!

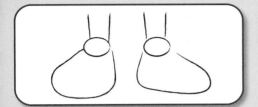

9. Now draw a rough semicircle around the end of each wrist. Add half a small sausage shape on the inside for the thumb and half an oval for the fingers.

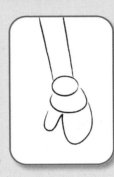

10. To start the face, draw some guidelines very lightly – one straight across the face, just below the circle, another straight down the middle.

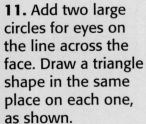

11. Add two large circles for eyes on the line across the face. Draw a triangle shape in the same place on each one, as shown.

12. Draw two small 'pip' shapes either side of the centre line for nostrils and a little semi-circle below that for the mouth. Don't forget to add your eyebrows!

13. Check your photo again to see what your hair is like – is it straight, curly or wavy? Where is your parting?

Start drawing your hair by adding a large curve around the head from each end of the line across your face.

14. Add a line for your parting and smooth, wavy or zigzag lines from the parting, out to the side.

15. Now it's time to add your clothes. Clothing is usually much bulkier than the frame of your body, so draw long lines away from your legs and arms for trousers and a top.

16. Once you are satisfied with how your Manga self looks, you need to go over the outlines in black pen.

17. When you get to the eyes, fill the whole circle with black except for the little triangle – this will then look like light reflecting in the eyes.

18. Leave the black pen to dry thoroughly and then carefully erase the pencil guidelines leaving just the black outline.

19. Finally, colour in your Manga character.

Gross History

People of the past had some horrible habits.
Read on to find out some of the filthiest
facts from history. Yuck!

FANTASTIC TOILETS!

Can you imagine what life would be like today without toilets? Looking back in time to the 1800s can give us the answer – it would be really, really disgusting. Flushing toilets did not appear until the late 19th century, and before they were invented people used to do their business in chamber pots, which then had to be emptied.

One of the common ways to do this was to open the window, shout, 'gardyloo!' and throw the contents into the street below. Charming!

London, in England, was a particularly stinky city. Up until the middle of the 19th century, most of London's untreated sewage ran into the River Thames. Sewage filled the streets and overflowed into the houses.

In 1858, after a very hot summer, the stench was so bad that the curtains in the Houses of Parliament, which is on the banks of the Thames, had to be soaked in a chemical called chlorine to hide the smell. The stench was known as 'The Great Stink', and this, coupled with the frequent outbreak of fatal diseases such as cholera, pushed the government into looking for a solution.

In the 1860s, an engineer named Joseph Bazalgette devised a network of underground sewers to transport the sewage out of the city and help beat back the stench. Much of Bazalgette's wide, brick sewer pipes are still in use today.

REVOLTING AMPUTATIONS

Before anaesthetics were invented to numb the pain of operations, the experience was horrific, not only for the patient but also for the surgeon and his team. Knives were used to cut into the flesh and then the bone was sawn through. This often needed two attempts as the first saw became too blunt. Afterwards, the wound was 'cauterized' by being burned with a red-hot iron to seal it. The pain was so intense that often patients had to be held down by four or five strong men.

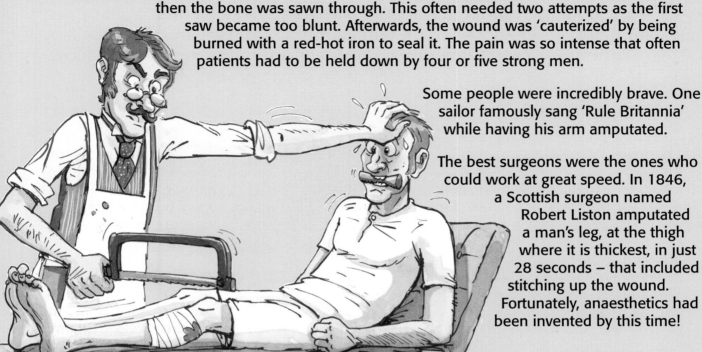

Some people were incredibly brave. One sailor famously sang 'Rule Britannia' while having his arm amputated.

The best surgeons were the ones who could work at great speed. In 1846, a Scottish surgeon named Robert Liston amputated a man's leg, at the thigh where it is thickest, in just 28 seconds – that included stitching up the wound. Fortunately, anaesthetics had been invented by this time!

BEASTLY BEHEADINGS

In 1587, Queen Elizabeth I of England signed the death warrant of her cousin, Mary Queen of Scots, when she discovered Mary was involved in a plot to get rid of her.

Mary's execution took place in Fotheringay Castle in Northamptonshire, England, where she had been imprisoned. In Tudor times there were three main methods of execution – being hanged, being burned at the stake and being beheaded. Being beheaded was considered the quickest of the three, but it didn't always go to plan, as poor Mary's story shows.

Mary was led to a scaffold in the castle hall, wearing only her petticoat.

After being blindfolded, Mary knelt, placed her head on the block and stretched her arms out behind her.

The first blow of the axe missed her neck and struck her on the back of the head. The second severed the neck except for a small bit of gristle which the executioner had to saw off. He then picked up Mary's severed head by her long hair and shouted, 'God save The Queen'. However the hair turned out to be a wig and Mary's head fell to the ground. Mary's lips moved for a quarter of an hour after her head had been chopped off. When they moved the body, her little pet dog was found hiding under her petticoat, unwilling to leave his mistress.

Snowy Survival

Try to imagine what it would be like to go trekking in Antarctica. The temperature would be −30°C and, if a blizzard blew up, winds of nearly 160 kilometres per hour might rip your tent out of the ground and blow it away. Here's what to do to survive the night.

EMERGENCY SNOW HOLE

You have to get out of the cold or you are not going to survive for more than a couple of hours.

There's no time to build a snow house or an igloo, but a snow hole can be built quickly and might save your life – all you need is a shovel.

Step 1.
Look for a suitable spot to dig your snow hole. A deep snow drift against a rock face is the best place to try – you can tunnel into it easily and there should be plenty of snow to shape into a good-sized shelter.

Step 2.
Make sure that the snow forming the drift isn't too powdery – you don't want the whole thing to cave in on you. Check the direction of the wind before you start digging. It should not be blowing directly towards you or your shelter will be very chilly.

Step 3.
Dig a tunnel, about a metre long, into the side of the snow drift. This will be the entrance to your snow hole, so it should be wide enough for you to crawl into it easily.

Step 4.
Crawl into the tunnel and begin to widen it out into a chamber large enough for you to lie down in comfortably. Be careful not to make the walls too thin, or your snow hole will fall in on you!

Step 5.
To be sure of an even cozier night, use some of the snow you have dug out to build a raised platform to curl up on, 20 to 30 centimetres high. Cold air is heavier than warm air, so it will be warmer on the platform than on the floor.

Step 6.
Before crawling into the snow hole, place something highly visible on the top of the shelter so that rescuers can find you easily. A pair of crossed ski poles is ideal, if you have them.

Step 7.
Pull your belongings into the hole with you. Don't forget your shovel in case you need to dig yourself out again. When you are inside, prop your rucksack against the entrance hole to keep out the wind.

Step 8.
Poke a small hole through the top of your shelter for ventilation, particularly if you are going to light a camping stove or candles.

Step 9.
Smooth out any lumps on the ceiling of your snow hole to prevent drips forming on them as the heat of your body raises the temperature inside.

Step 10.
If you have anything waterproof, wrap it round your sleeping bag before you get in, to prevent you getting wet and to keep you extra warm. Wear as many clothes as you can – several layers will help to keep you warm through the night.

Step 11.
While you are waiting for the blizzard to pass, it's a good idea to eat to give your body more energy to heat itself.

Step 12.
When the air is below freezing, even breathing causes the body to lose water, so it's vital to keep yourself properly hydrated by drinking plenty of water.

Now it's time to settle down for a good night's rest until rescue arrives – pleasant dreams!

Antarctic Explorers

Antarctica is one of the most difficult places to survive on earth. Captain Robert Falcon Scott led an expedition to find out more about this fascinating continent. Read on to discover more about his heroic and tragic adventure.

Captain Scott was an officer in the Royal Navy. In June 1910, he made a second attempt to lead an expedition to reach the South Pole.

Antarctica has very extreme weather. Even in summer, temperatures drop to below −30°C and winds can reach up to 160 kilometres per hour. Nonetheless, Scott anchored his ship, selected 11 men, and began the long, cold journey with motorized sledges, dogs and ponies.

Dangerous territory

The trek to the Pole had many problems. The motors on their sledges broke, so the men had to haul them themselves, which was exhausting. The ponies couldn't take the cold conditions and many of them died. The teams of dogs had to be sent back to base camp. The men were suffering so much that Captain Scott sent seven of them back to base and he was forced to continue on to the Pole with only four companions.

After 81 days of trekking, the five brave men finally reached the Pole. But they were dealt a blow when they saw that a Norwegian, named Roald Amundsen, had got there before them.

Disappointed and weary, the British team put their flag next to the Norwegian flag, then began the return journey. But the Antarctic winter was beginning. The temperatures dropped even further and fierce blizzards made the journey almost impossible.

One member of the team died a month after their arrival at the Pole and by the middle of March, one of Scott's men, Captain Oates, had such bad frostbite in his feet that he could hardly walk. He chose to sacrifice himself, going out into the snow in his socks, so that the others could continue without him. Sadly, his heroic gesture was in vain. The remaining men died in their tent a few days later – they were just a few kilometres from a supply hut. Captain Scott wrote a final entry in his diary, '…the end cannot be far. It seems a pity, but I do not think I can write more.'

Tragedy strikes

The tent was found eight months later. Scott's diary and photographs gave a fascinating account of the bravery and endurance of this small group of men who had conquered the Antarctic.

Out Of This World?

See how spectacular your knowledge of the solar system is in this cool quiz. Check your answers on page 60.

1. What is the explosion caused by a dying star called?

A. Superduper.
B. Supernova.
C. Supersundae.

2. Why do planets orbit the sun?

A. They are attracted by the Sun's heat.
B. The Sun's gravity holds them in place.
C. Strong solar winds keep them in orbit.

3. What is the giant red spot on the surface of Jupiter?

A. A constant, powerful storm.
B. A huge swimming pool.
C. An alien city.

4. Why is Mars called the 'Red Planet'?

A. Violent winds and storms whip up clouds of fiery gas.
B. Because the rocks contain a red rust called iron oxide.
C. Because it's so hot it glows like a fire.

5. Why are comets also known as 'dirty snowballs'?

A. They are wet and slushy.
B. They hurt if they hit you.
C. They are made of ice and surrounded by gas and dust.

6. The Aurora Borealis is an amazing sight – what is it?

A. The brightest star in the Solar System.
B. Highly charged electrons entering the Earth's atmosphere.
C. A massive wave caused by the full moon.

7. When the toilet on the International Space Station broke, what did the astronauts do?

A. Urinated out of the window.
B. Crossed their legs until they could return home.
C. Used specially designed urine-collection bags until it could be fixed.

8. The Romans named the planets after their gods. Mars was god of war, Venus was the goddess of love, but what was Saturn god of?

A. The god of satellite television.
B. The god of sandwiches.
C. The god of time.

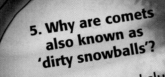
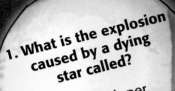

Amazing Astronomy

On a clear night, the sky is full of stars and lots of them are easy to find, even without a telescope or pair of binoculars. Read on to discover how you can become a stargazing astronomer at home.

Constellations

Many groups of stars form patterns, called 'constellations'. It takes a year for the Earth to travel round the sun, bringing different stars into view during different months.

Here are some of the best constellations to look for and when you can see them. You need to check which way north, south, east and west are at your house. Check this on a map of your local area – north is at the top of the page – or you can use a compass, if you have one.

TAURUS

The shape of this constellation is thought to have been shown in cave paintings as far back as 13,000BC!

Pleiades

Taurus moves east to west across the sky between September and March in the Northern Hemisphere – the half of the planet which is above the equator. First find Orion (see below), then look out for the V-shape above and to the right of Orion – this is the bull's face. A cluster of seven bright stars sits on the bull's shoulder. These are called the *Pleiades*, or Seven Sisters. The ancient Greeks believed these were the seven daughters of the god Atlas, said to have been placed in the sky by Zeus, the king of the gods, to escape Orion. However, he put them in the wrong place – the two constellations, Orion and Taurus, are side by side.

Orion's Belt

ORION

Orion and the scorpion – the constellation, Scorpio – were enemies in Greek mythology. They were placed at opposite ends of the sky to make sure that they never meet.

Between September and March in the Northern Hemisphere, Orion the Hunter is easy to find because of the row of three stars known as 'Orion's belt'. Face east and look to your right. Orion is the brightest constellation in the sky, so you should also be able to find four bright stars around the belt. From the bottom left (Orion's foot) and moving clockwise, these are called Saiph, Betelgeuse, Bellatrix and Rigel.

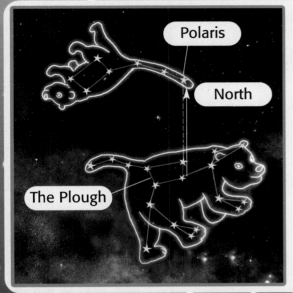

URSA MAJOR AND URSA MINOR

Ursa Major, or the Great Bear, can be seen throughout the year. The most famous group of stars in Ursa Major are known as the Plough, or the Big Dipper, because they make a shape a little like a ladle or 'dipper'. If you draw a line through its two brightest stars (on the right when viewed from the angle shown), the line 'points' to Polaris. This star is also known as the North Star because it stays in the same place in the sky and always points north. Polaris is at the tip of the tail of Ursa Minor, or the Little Bear, also known as the Little Dipper.

In Greek mythology, a woman named Callisto and her son, Arcas, were both turned into bears. They were flung into the sky by Zeus, who swung them round and round by their short tails, stretching them into the long shape you can see now.

PEGASUS

Pegasus is the winged horse of Greek mythology. It can be seen from September to January in the Northern Hemisphere. To find it, first look for Ursa Major (see above).

Use the pointer stars to find Polaris, then follow the line through it. You'll pass a constellation shaped like a 'W', or an 'M', depending on which way you look at it, called Cassiopeia. Past this is Pegasus. Look for the box-shape, which is the body of the horse. You should spot the strands of stars that make up the head and the neck of the horse and two of its legs.

Pegasus is only the right way up when it is in the Southern Hemisphere, so turn this book around to check the pattern of stars you are looking for.

Did you know?

All together there are 88 constellations. The smallest is in the Southern Hemisphere – the half of the earth that is below the equator – and can only occasionally be seen just above the equator. It is called the Southern Cross, or *Crux Australis*. Its cross-shape is shown on the national flag of Australia, New Zealand and Brazil.

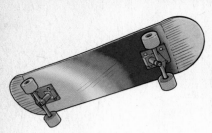
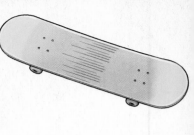

Skater Boy

Skateboarding is one of the coolest sports around. These moves look pretty impressive and are great fun to do, so grab your board and get practising.

HOW TO DO AN OLLIE

Start by doing a stationary Ollie, until you've cracked the technique, then move on to tackle jumps and obstacles.

1. Position your feet on the board, so that the ball of your back foot is resting on the tail of the board and your front foot is in the centre.

2. Bend your knees ready to jump. Push down sharply on the tail of the board with your back foot.

3. Immediately straighten your legs as though jumping into the air. The pressure you have put on the back of the board will make the front of the board stay with your foot.

4. As the board comes up, slide your front foot towards the nose of the skateboard and push down.

5. Bend your back knee towards your chest to allow the tail of the board to come up. The board will now be level in the air.

6. As you come down, bend your legs to absorb the impact of landing.

Add your own cool design to the bottom of this skateboard.

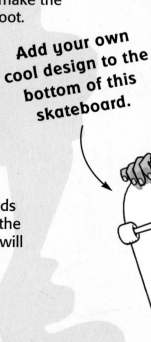

Once you can do an Ollie, you're ready to try some more tricks. Here are a couple to get you started.

THE MANUAL

A manual on a skateboard is a bit like a wheelie on a bike. When performed correctly it allows you to travel along on just the back two wheels of your skateboard. Here's how:

1. Build up a pretty good speed and cover the tail end of your board with your back foot. Put your front foot on the front screws.

2. Slowly shift your weight to the back foot while leaning forward. The nose of the board will come up. Whatever you do, don't lean backwards or you will fall off!

3. You may feel as though you are losing balance, so hold out your arms as though you were on a tight-rope as you roll along.

4. To finish, shift your weight back to the front foot and put the front wheels down.

THE KICK FLIP

A kick flip looks really good if you get it right, but it's a tricky one to land, so practise on grass first to beat those bruises!

Top tip
Practise, practise, practise!

1. Put your back foot on the tail end of the board. Place your front foot so that your toes are over the screws or bolts, and your heel hangs off the board.

2. Bend your knees and push down on the end of the board with your back foot, then slide your front foot up the board like in an Ollie.

3. As your front foot reaches the nose of the board, flick your foot off the end of it so that the board rotates all the way around, lengthways.

4. When the board is the right way up again, catch it with both feet and land squarely on both sets of wheels, bending your knees as you land.

Going For Gold

The hunt for gold has inspired hundreds of people, from intrepid explorers to bloodthirsty pirates. Read on to find out about a legendary city of gold, and discover more about this precious and beautiful metal.

CITY OF GOLD

There is a legend that somewhere in South America is a city of gold called El Dorado. It has been the dream of every explorer, since the 16th century, to find this legendary place and plunder its wealth for themselves.

The myth of El Dorado started long ago, when a native tribe of South Americans began telling stories about an ancient ceremony that took place at Lake Guatavita, north of the city of Bogotá in Colombia.

The name 'El Dorado' comes from this ceremony, which was held whenever a new king came to power. First, the king was stripped and covered from head to foot with powdered gold. Then, he stood on a raft while heaps of gold and jewels were piled at his feet.

The new leader threw the dazzling riches into the lake to please a god that lived under the water. The shining, gold-covered king was known as 'El Dorado', which means 'the gilded one' in Spanish.

This ceremony happened over and over again until the late 15th century. The lake was supposed to be filled to the brim with the most fantastic treasures.

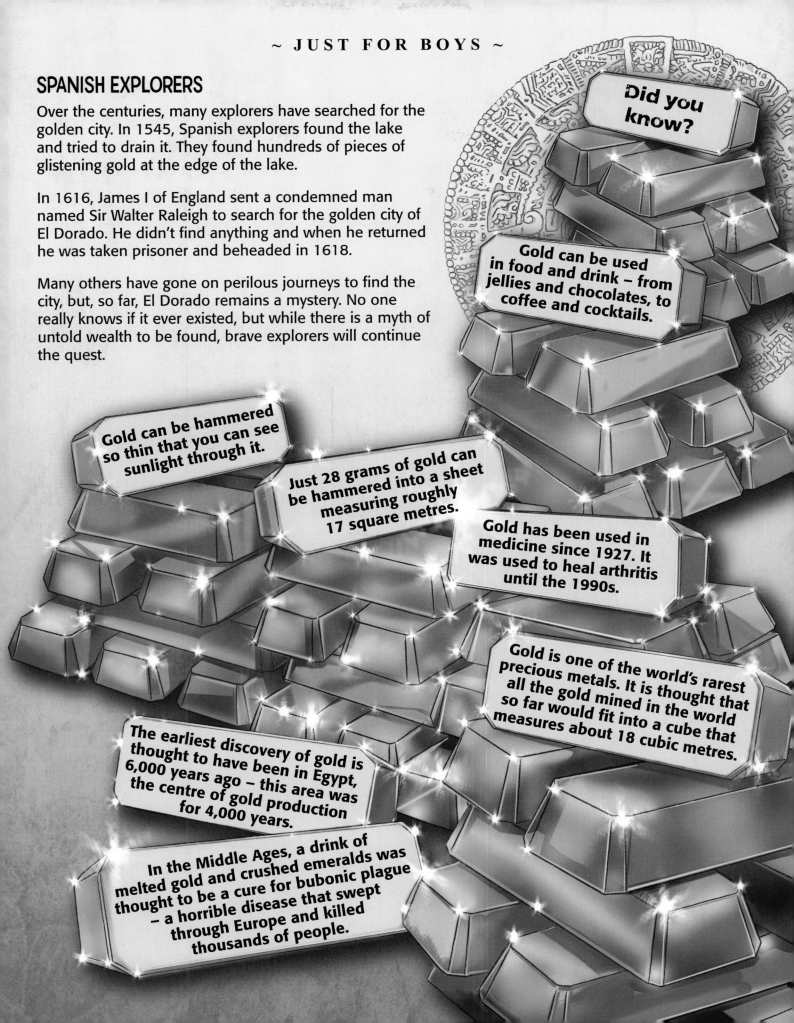

SPANISH EXPLORERS

Over the centuries, many explorers have searched for the golden city. In 1545, Spanish explorers found the lake and tried to drain it. They found hundreds of pieces of glistening gold at the edge of the lake.

In 1616, James I of England sent a condemned man named Sir Walter Raleigh to search for the golden city of El Dorado. He didn't find anything and when he returned he was taken prisoner and beheaded in 1618.

Many others have gone on perilous journeys to find the city, but, so far, El Dorado remains a mystery. No one really knows if it ever existed, but while there is a myth of untold wealth to be found, brave explorers will continue the quest.

Did you know?

Gold can be used in food and drink – from jellies and chocolates, to coffee and cocktails.

Gold can be hammered so thin that you can see sunlight through it.

Just 28 grams of gold can be hammered into a sheet measuring roughly 17 square metres.

Gold has been used in medicine since 1927. It was used to heal arthritis until the 1990s.

Gold is one of the world's rarest precious metals. It is thought that all the gold mined in the world so far would fit into a cube that measures about 18 cubic metres.

The earliest discovery of gold is thought to have been in Egypt, 6,000 years ago – this area was the centre of gold production for 4,000 years.

In the Middle Ages, a drink of melted gold and crushed emeralds was thought to be a cure for bubonic plague – a horrible disease that swept through Europe and killed thousands of people.

Aztec Adventure

Enter the ancient world of the amazing Aztecs and see if you have what it takes to solve these puzzles. Turn to page 61 to find out the answers.

SYMBOL SPOTTER

Can you spot two of each of these symbols in the Aztec marketplace below?

MATCHING GODS

Which gods do not have an exact pair?

1

2

3

4

5

6

7

8

AZTEC CALENDAR DISC

Only one set of pieces will complete the disk.
Is it **A**, **B**, **C** or **D**?

A

B

C

D

MIND-BOGGLING MAZE

Can you find your way to the sun
disk at the top of the pyramid?

START

The Spy Files

Top-secret spies need top-secret codes to keep information to themselves. Whether you're swooping in to save the day or meeting friends at the park, use the codes and top code-cracking tips on these pages to pass details of your plans between the members of your own spy ring (or friends).

PEN SPIRALS

What looks like an innocent strip of paper to most people can actually be a secret message that only you and your friends will know how to unlock. Here's how:

1. Use a ruler to measure a strip of paper ½ cm wide and 25 cm long. Cut it out.

2. Wrap the strip round a pen in a spiral and write your secret message on it.

3. When you unwrap the pen spiral, whatever you have written on it will just look like mysterious squiggles – except to anyone you've let in on the secret.

4. Make sure that anyone who needs to read your message has a pen identical to yours. They will then be able to wrap the strip around their own pen to read your message.

MAD-SPEAK

A secret language, such as 'Pig Latin', where an 'ay' sound is added to the end of each word to disguise it, is often the best way to keep things between friends. That way you can even carry on a conversation in front of unsuspecting adults. Here's how:

1. For words beginning with a vowel – A, E, I, O or U – just add the 'ay' sound to the end. So 'and' becomes 'and-ay', 'even' becomes 'even-ay' and 'if' becomes 'if-ay'.

2. If a word begins with a consonant – any of the other letters of the alphabet – move the first letter to the end of the word, then add the 'ay' sound. For instance, 'win' becomes 'in-way', 'jump' becomes 'ump-jay' and so on.

3. Lastly, if a word begins with two consonants such as 'br-' or 'cl-', move them both to the end of the word, then add the 'ay' sound. So 'break' becomes 'eak-bray' and 'click' becomes 'ick-clay'.

If you speak fast enough, no one will have any idea what you're saying!

ALPHASHIFT

A substitution code is one of the simplest ways of disguising a secret message. Here's how:

• In a substitution code you simply swap each letter for another. For example, this sentence, 'J bn uif hsfbuftu tqz fwfs,' has been made by swapping each letter from the original sentence for the next letter in the alphabet. So A has been swapped for B, B for C, C for D and so on.

• To decode this sentence, swap each letter for the one that comes before it in the alphabet. Can you work out what the coded sentence says? The answer is on page 61.

• To disguise your own messages, you can use this code or choose another – for instance, you could swap each letter for one five, seven or nine letters later.

SOGGY SECRETS

Here's an easy way to make your writing invisible:

1. First lay a plastic bag over your writing surface to keep it dry. Then you'll need two sheets of paper that are the same size and a pencil.

2. Fill a sink with enough water to dunk just one of the sheets of paper in.

3. Wet it quickly and lay it on your writing surface, over the bag.

4. Lay the dry sheet of paper over the top, write your message and then peel it away.

5. Discard the top sheet and leave the bottom sheet to dry. Once dry, the writing will it disappear, but will reappear as soon as the paper is wet again.

TOP SECRET!

MARK'S MYSTERIOUS HOLIDAY

Calling all mystery detectives! Can you spot how many objects
Mrs Carruthers try to steal in the story? Turn to page 61 to find out.

Line-Up Logic

These six people are potential suspects in a diamond theft at a local museum. Use the clues below to work out who is responsible. You'll find the answer on page 61.

1. A strand of blond hair was discovered inside the cabinet, where the diamond had been sitting.

2. An eyewitness described a person of, 'at least 180 centimetres in height' running down an alley at the side of the museum, immediately after the alarm went off.

3. A small amount of blood was found along the edge of the cabinet door.

4. Finally, several large trainer footprints were found leading away from the cabinet where the diamond was displayed.

Terracotta Army

The Terracotta Army is one of the most spectacular archaeological discoveries ever. Read on to find out about this amazing find.

In 1974, some farmers were digging in a field in China, when they uncovered a huge underground chamber. This chamber was part of the tomb of the First Sovereign Emperor, Qin Shi Huang, who united China under his rule in 221BC. But it was what was found in the chamber that amazed everyone. Thousands of life-sized terracotta clay soldiers were lined up, ready to protect the dead emperor on his journey into the afterlife.

An amazing find

The incredible thing about these soldiers was that each one was unique. Some had beards, some looked stern, others were cheerful. The hair, nose, mouth and eyes of each one were different. There were archers carrying bows and arrows, and foot soldiers with daggers and spears.

Some figures had swords and longbows, others had axes. Their weapons had been coated in a special metal, which had stopped them from rusting. After being buried for over 2,000 years, they were still as sharp and as shiny as ever.

Three massive vaults of soldiers have since been uncovered, all quite close to each other.

Yet to be discovered

Archaeologists originally thought that the tomb in which the Emperor is buried must have been destroyed, but they now think that the discovery of the army makes this unlikely. The tomb is said to be so enormous that it took 700,000 men to construct it.

Historical records from Ancient China say that the tomb is filled with golden palaces, trees are made of precious jade and filled with gold and silver birds. There are mechanical crossbows that are triggered to fire at intruders, rivers and seas are made to flow with silvery liquid mercury, and the lamps are filled with whale oil to make them burn for many years.

Tests done on the soil near the vaults have shown traces of mercury, so it may not be long before this amazing tomb is discovered.

Treasure Seekers

You're on an important dig with a group of archaeologists, hunting for hidden treasure. In the grid below are three swords, four terracotta soldiers and five shields. However, only two swords, two soldiers and three shields have been found so far. Your job is to uncover the remaining treasures.

You must find the remaining sword, two soldiers and two shields. The numbers on the grid tell you how many squares or groups of squares are occupied in each row or column. For example, the numbers **3** and **1** by the top row tell you that a group of three squares together and one square by itself are occupied, with one empty square or more in between. The soldier in this row occupies three squares together, then after a gap of four squares there is a shield by itself.

Use the other numbers by the rows and columns to help you work out where the remaining treasures are. You'll find the answer on page 61. Good luck.

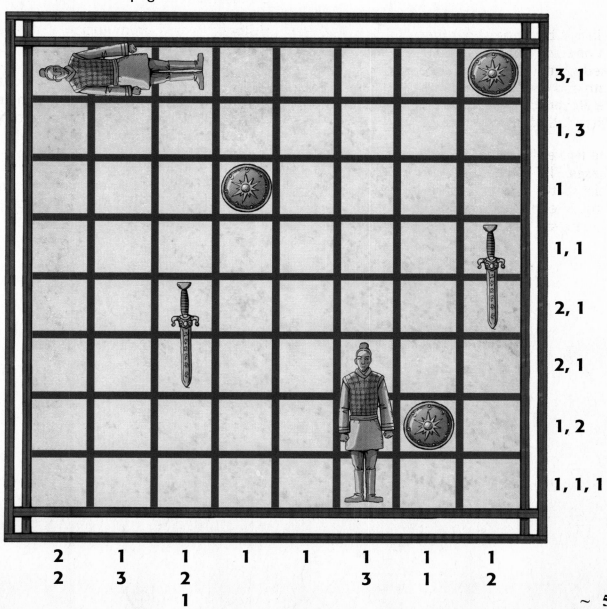

Tomb Tactics

You're trapped in a Chinese emperor's tomb and must race to be the first to escape! Grab a dice, and a counter for each player. Place all the counters on 'Start' – whoever rolls the highest number goes first – then follow the instructions on the board to get to the 'Finish' and freedom!

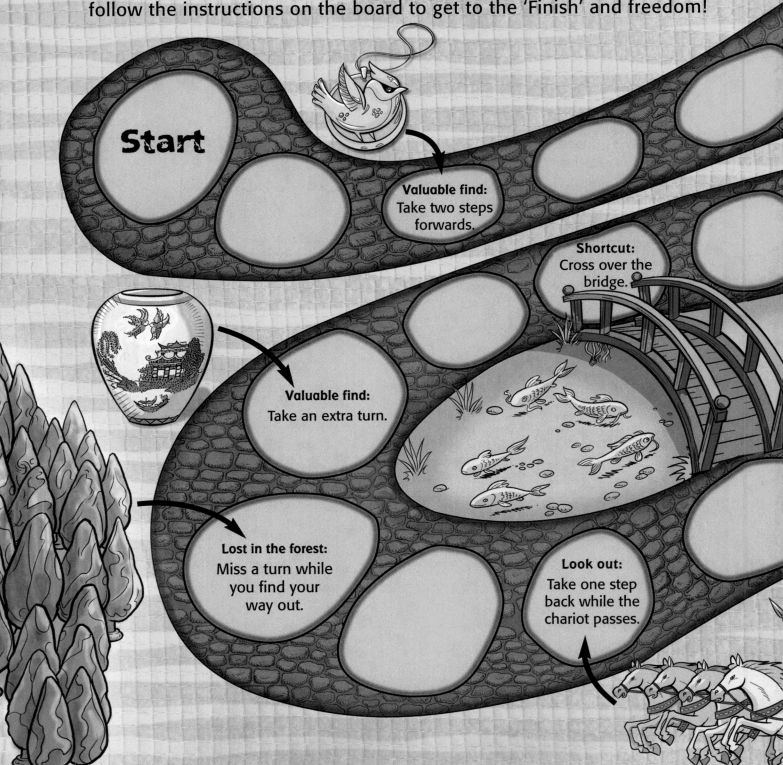

Start

Valuable find: Take two steps forwards.

Shortcut: Cross over the bridge.

Valuable find: Take an extra turn.

Lost in the forest: Miss a turn while you find your way out.

Look out: Take one step back while the chariot passes.

Under attack:
Run back
three steps.

Found:
A lamp to light
your way –
move two steps
forward.

Under attack:
Miss a turn while
you disable the
crossbow.

Slipped
in the lake:
Join the nearest
player on the
board.

Uh oh:
You've left something
behind – go back
across the log.

Valuable find:
Take an extra
turn.

Finish

Caught in a trap:
Throw a six to
escape.

Answers

WEIRD NATURE (PAGE 10)

Did you spot that the story about Morocco's climbing rabbits was the sneaky lie? The rabbits in Morocco keep their thumping feet firmly on the ground, preferring to snack on grass. However, the branches of the argan trees of Morocco *can* sometimes be filled with goats. These goats love the argan fruit, and use their agile climbing skills to reach it.

THE HAUNTED HOUSE (PAGES 20 - 21)

THE ROOM OF MYSTERIES

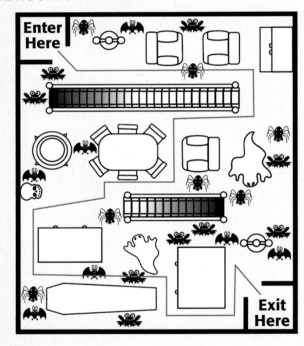

SPOOKDOKU

1	4	2	3
2	3	1	4
3	1	4	2
4	2	3	1

SKELE-DANCE

CREEPTANGULAR

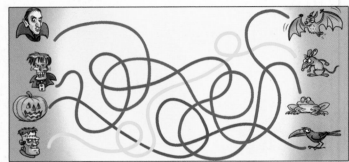

OUTBACK PUZZLER (PAGE 22)

USELESS INVENTIONS (PAGES 32 - 33)

The Trouser Chair and the Fish Toilet are the two fake inventions. However, a real aquarium is available that wraps around the toilet cistern (the part that holds the water) rather than the poor fish swimming around in the bowl eating poop. All the other bonkers brainwaves are real!

OUT OF THIS WORLD? (PAGE 41)

1. B **2.** B **3.** A **4.** B **5.** C **6.** B **7.** C **8.** C

AZTEC ADVENTURE (PAGES 48 - 49)

MATCHING GODS

Spot the difference? Gods 3 and 4 each have a differently coloured collar. All the others are the same.

3   4

AZTEC CALENDAR DISC

The correct set of pieces is group **A**.

MIND-BOGGLING MAZE

THE SPY FILES (PAGE 51)

ALPHASHIFT

The sentence reads, 'I am the greatest spy ever.'

MARK'S MYSTERIOUS HOLIDAY (PAGES 52 - 54)

Tick each of the items that you noticed disappearing from Castle Ballantyne.

Mark's favourite game	☐
The candlestick	☐
The vase	☐
The teapot	☐
The pair of goblets	☐
A painting	☐
The good cutlery	☐
The statues on the mantlepiece	☐

LINE-UP LOGIC (PAGE 55)

TREASURE SEEKERS (PAGE 57)

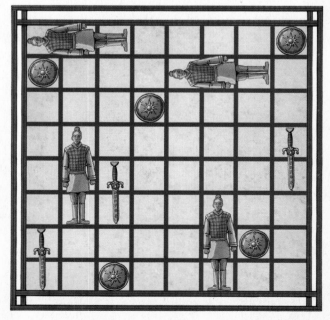